Charles Wehrenberg

MISSISSIPPI BLUE

Henry P. Bosse and his Views on the Mississippi River

Between Minneapolis and St. Louis, 1883–1891

Twin Palms Publishers 2002

Contents

For my father

Paul Henry Wehrenberg

who shared his love

for the water

Henry P. Bosse

[1844–1903]

American Impressionist

I CAME TO COLLECT old maps from an interest in fine books. That was in 1969. My favorite antiquarian, Giovanni Scopazzi of San Francisco, sold me on the idea of travelling through time with his precious maps and voyages. The sixteenth century came alive with the genius of Ortelius, Plantin and Peter Bruegel of Antwerp, King Philip II of Spain, and Nicolas Monardes of Seville. I loved those conversations, often over a dinner of succulent salmon quenelles and copious bottles of French champagne. The Northwest Passage, New World plants, exotic islands like Japan, Galapagos, Los Bolcanes . . . the flat Earth was becoming a globe. The old maps brought to life an age of discovery unequalled until our own with its photographic maps of our moon and Mars, and its map of the human genome. Scopazzi's European savoir faire animated his feeling for the human spirit, for its desire to explore and chronicle, and for creativity's odd way of compounding science with art. Of course, we had our differences: Scopazzi disdained my interest in photography as thoroughly tedious. For Giovanni, humanity realized its highest potential with a perfectly conceived map, especially the richly illustrated gems of the sixteenth and seventeenth centuries.

As much as I enjoyed thinking about sixteenth-century Antwerp and the atlases of the Familists, I continued to wonder where photography had first made an impact on cartography. Laussedat's survey of Paris in 1864 is said to have been the first application of photography to map making, although Nadar had been pressing the case for its use since the 1850s. Clearly, landscape and survey photography began with the camera, but my interest was more particular. Some nuance of discovery is a key to making an important map. Still, is it not simply visual appeal that makes certain maps so special? How might all this come together in a photographic iteration? Just how might a serious cartographer use photography to chart new water, so to speak? It seemed to demand an entirely new look, one considerable in terms of earlier decorative maps solely in that the photographic map must have enduring visual appeal, a look that continues to tie human curiosity and aspiration to the land and the water.

One day in 1990, while leafing through a Sotheby's auction catalog, I came across a photograph that riveted my attention. An old cyanotype, it was a blue oval that seemed to float on the page like a bubble. It portrayed proud men on a boat, a river dredge that I would come to know as the *Phoenix*. On the facing page, a second cyanotype reflected on man's folly as a river inundated a town. Modern and postmodern, comedy and tragedy juxtaposed, they were illuminated as much by the light off the water as the light from the sky.

The flooded town brought back memories. I was born in Saint Louis and grew up in Indiana. Near my childhood home, streams gathered into rivers large enough for boats, rivers powerful enough to become water that goes somewhere. The water made the corn and grass grow, and it promised escape. It also flooded our basement on occasion . . . as it had inundated the town in the old photograph up for auction.

The cyanotypes were part of an album depicting the Mississippi River between Minneapolis and St. Louis. I had never heard of the photographer, an unknown named Henry P. Bosse. The images simply spoke for themselves. The leather-bound volume, fifteen by seventeen inches, held 169 dreamy blue images in all. On the cover, embossed in gold, the title read *Views on Upper Mississippi River*. (The highly decorated inside title page, also a cyanotype print, read *Views on the Mississippi River between Minneapolis, Minn. and St. Louis, Mo.*/From negatives taken and printed under the direction of Major A. Mackenzie, Corps of Engineers U.S.A./ by/H. Bosse, Draughtsman/1883–1891.) I had to have it. And that, of course, ended up costing me a small fortune.

The dates in the album began in 1883 and continued into 1893, overlapping French Impressionism in Europe and ending as Claude Monet painted the *Rouen Cathedral*, and Claude Debussy finished *Prélude à l'après-midi d'un faune*. The world was becoming a more complex place as Asia, Europe, and the Americas accelerated into modern times. Henry Bosse and Claude Debussy were part of the action. Debussy's quintessential work of impressionistic music was first performed in Paris as Henry Bosse's cyanotypes made their debut in Chicago. It is unlikely they knew of one another. One day, while listening to music by Debussy, I happened to watch Bosse's *Views on the Mississippi River* on my TV from a photo CD that I had made. André Previn was conducting the London Symphonic Orchestra as I floated down the Mississippi with Henry Bosse. Debussy and Bosse seemed a perfect fit. It made me think of Bosse in the context of his times, the news he might have heard, the music of his day.

Since acquiring Bosse's photographic essay, I have studied it thoroughly and uncovered what I could about this amazing man. While Henry Bosse remains enigmatic, I've come to regard his masterpieces as major works of American impressionism, a landmark in cartography, and a magnificent emblem of Midwestern creativity.

Because each person is shaped by a past and a present, I have included several articles that informed Henry Bosse's contemporary reality (see "Bosse's World"). Windows into his world, they allow him to speak for himself, as a man of his times. He is the confluence, if you will, of the European eye, with which he began, and the expressive intentions that he nurtured, subsequently, to define himself.

Not much is known about Henry Peter Bosse. Born in Germany in 1844, he may have been the son of an unmarried daughter of the prominent Gneisenau family and that family's tutor. He entered the United States in 1865 and worked in stationery stores in Chicago, dealers in printed books, fine prints, and frames, in addition to paper and ink. Letters and cards suggest that Bosse liked to drink, sing, and play cards, but he was a sophisticated man by American standards, the grandson of the Prussian

Henry P. Bosse, circa 1900. Photographer unknown
Courtesy William Quaintance, Moline, Illinois

general credited with the strategy that defeated Napoleon at Waterloo. He was also a man of humor: he photographed his dog dressed as a card player, and drew a cartoon of himself as Tom Sawyer, floating the river in a tub with a tripod camera.

John Anfinson, formerly the Saint Paul district historian for the U.S. Army Corps of Engineers, explains the circumstances that led Bosse to photograph the river: "Before the U.S. Army Corps of Engineers could begin remaking the upper Mississippi River, it needed to understand the river better. So during the winter of 1877–78, Major Francis U. Farquhar, the Rock Island District commander, directed his engineers to synthesize all the earlier river maps into a general map of the upper Mississippi from St. Anthony Falls to Grafton. When completed, the new map included 26 sheets. Not satisfied with the map's detail and coverage, Farquhar asked the Chief of Engineers for $60,000 to resurvey the river, and on July 8, 1878, the chief approved. To draw the new map, Major Farquhar needed a talented draftsman. Farquhar had been the St. Paul district engineer from 1873–78, and Bosse had worked for St. Paul in 1875 and maybe longer. Knowing Bosse's skills, Farquhar probably asked him to move to Rock Island."

Bosse knew that no line-drawn map would suffice, because the river was forever changing and wild. His map would have to convey a feel for the way of the water and the lay of the land. His goal was to leave a lasting impression of the Mississippi as part of the American dream, revealing both what was and what was to come. Considered north to south, his *Views* are a grand ride down the Mississippi, a navigable view from the land and the water. The whole is a map more easily followed than any drawn map. Bosse's sequence, however, is not strictly ordered north to south in the Mackenzie album.

As an atlas, Henry Bosse's *Views on the Mississippi River* is more than a classical map augmented by photographic views. A drawn map is inherently idealized, static. Bosse's river is the water itself, moving, forever changing, a sequence of encounters and tides, rising and falling. Bosse went far beyond illustration, especially when he printed his detailed negatives as blue-on-white ovals. Like the great atlases of Ortelius and Blæu, Bosse's album is inspirational. After its publication, there could be no doubt that photography would redefine cartography. Bosse made his profession something more, as did his contemporary Monet when he took French painting one step beyond the conventional.

While there were impressionistic paintings before Claude Monet, it was he who made the Impressionistic mood prevail in painting. As a specific art movement, Impressionism is relevant to Henry Bosse because it defines his times. Obviously, Henry Bosse can never be construed as a French Impressionist, but he resonated in America with the complex æsthetic that made Impressionism an enduring transcultural movement.

In his authoritative study of Monet, William Seitz tells us, "The precepts imparted by Boudin to his precocious student [Claude Monet] were unquestionably those that were recorded in his [Boudin's] own notebooks. Self-deprecatory in tone, they are nevertheless rich, clearly expressed, and revolutionary. Only careful study can reveal their commitment and almost pantheistic devotion to nature. Tormented by a sense of his own incapacity, Boudin pursued a 'perfection' of fleeting color and light that always eluded his technical grasp. He felt it was essential to retain 'one's first impression,' and discovered that everything that is painted directly and on the spot always has a force, a power, a vivacity of touch that cannot be recreated in the studio. Quite simply, Boudin put forward Impressionism's cardinal principle, thus elevating the sketch – with the inevitable premium that it places on concentrated observation and rapid execution – to the status of a completed work of art."

10

This assertion flew in the face of the status quo. The nineteenth century was dominated by meticulous studio painting that exalted an easy-to-appreciate realism. According to Barbara Rose in her essay "America as Paradise," American Luminism was a *retardataire*, naturalistic style that rejected Impressionism as a scientific, secular attitude toward landscape, incompatible with the Transcendentalist idea of nature as a metaphysical force of mysterious origin. She concludes, "Based on scientific observation, impressionionism reflected a modernist consciousness of nature dependent not on mystical illumination but on physical laws." Amid the confusion, photography continued to evolve steadily.

If, in the hands of an artist, a photograph is the equivalent of a sketch, then whether it is a work of art or mere quotidian document becomes a matter of the "feel" emanating from the print itself. Regarding Bosse's cyanotypes, color dominates the first impression. It excites an anticipation that greater detail would not, a feeling that infers Henry Bosse's intention. While Bosse set out to impart information, he first wanted the viewer to feel the environment in the hands of man, and sense the frailty of human ambition in the face of nature. The album seems more an opera than an arcane recitation of details. Indeed, it is this palpability of Bosse's impression that commands attention. Light seems to effervesce from the water itself. The images float on the pages, dense with information yet light in spirit.

From the moment one opens the album, it is immediately apparent that the artist meant the photographs to be more than a record of fact. Simply put, these photographs show more than work, they show a commitment to an aesthetic ideal. The work is a labor of love sustained over many years. Each of the images is meticulously composed. In each, a prescient unity is achieved.

Like the Mississippi itself, Bosse's distinctive style ties first to last, so that in the final cyanotype, one can hardly see the river. Nature has been erased. The modern river is about steel and machines, not water, and his romance with the modern reveals a very postmodern reality.

The aesthetic intelligence apparent in Bosse's *Views* exemplifies a well-expounded theme of the 1880s. William Morris lectured throughout England on the need for art in everyday life, creating an international cause célèbre in 1885 when he was tossed into jail for his protests against artless work and artlessly industrialized society. While he railed against the profit motive and the railway Philistines, Morris insisted on the need for art in every effort, for the sanity of self and society. Art, in this context, implies a pleasure in doing reflected in the final output. Art was that which added enjoyment to labor and allowed the output to become more venerable with age. This is exactly the issue addressed so powerfully by Henry Bosse's presentation of his *Views on the Mississippi River*. He wanted his contribution to be more than expedient, more than mere rectangles concerned only with depiction.

Henry Bosse knew about printing photographs in black and white. So, why blue on white? Why the ovals? What comes through Bosse's photographic essay is the consistency of a master and the intentionality of a visionary. Clearly, he had something very particular in mind. At a glance, beauty draws you into the order and chaos depicted. Bosse wanted you to come back again and again, allowing profound ironies and ever deeper layers of relevance to emerge. He was a man in touch with his own time and place, and he meant to leave his impression of it for all to see and feel. For me, as I leafed through the album the first time, and

Port of Dubuque. Henry Bosse
Photograph courtesy U.S. Army Corps of Engineers

every time since, Bosse's *Views* realize Oscar Wilde's sense of human potential: "It is impossible to have good workmanship unless the worker himself can see the beautiful things in Nature about him."

A word about Henry Bosse's known body of work. He produced something like 345 different cyanotype views of the Mississippi over a period of ten years. The precise number is difficult to assess. Variants are numbered A, B, etc., and occasionally there is no number at all. Some are cyanotypes, others albumen prints. And to make things more complex, on occasion, more than one glass plate negative was exposed, with minute differences distinguishing the prints. The Mackenzie album contained 169 of these cyanotype views, which form a detailed topographical map of the upper Mississippi. Each of the five known albums is unique. The prints vary in condition: the Mackenzie album prints are fine to extra fine.

The Mackenzie cyanotype album features the oval image motif, as does the Army Corps album in Saint Paul, and the Mayo Foundation album in Rochester. The Bosse album held by the Mississippi River Museum in Dubuque, Iowa, also has several panoramic foldouts, while the Rock Island Army Corps album employs a variety of image treatments from straight rectangular albumen prints to circles and ovals with wildly patterned borders that recall William Morris and Company wallpaper. Each album variant has a slightly different selection of views.

All of the Mackenzie album images are cyanotypes on off-white paper from negatives made between 1883 and 1893. Many sheets bear the watermark "Johannot et Cie Annonay, aloe's satino." The oval-masked images are each approximately 10.25 x 13 inches. The images are individually titled and dated in black ink by hand. The elegant handwriting suggests that Henry Bosse did the title calligraphy himself.

The discovery of the Mackenzie album of Henry Bosse cyanotypes is a great treasure-in-the-attic story. An antique dealer and amateur historian discovered the album in Washington, D.C., as he sold things from the estate of a daughter of Army Corps Chief of Engineers Alexander Mackenzie. More interested in Mackenzie's personal life and papers, the dealer donated most of the Bosse ephemera to the Army Corps Archive. The Mackenzie album of Bosse cyanotypes, however, was so obviously special that even someone with no interest in fine photography could see that it was a gem. The antique dealer brought the Mackenzie album to Sotheby's, where it sold at a record price for a then-

Lake Suwa in Shiano Province, from
Thirty-Six Views of Mt. Fuji, 1825–1832. Katsushika Hokusai
Woodblock print courtesy Rijksmuseum, Amsterdam

unknown photographer. Fortunately, the dealer also brought Bosse to the attention of the historian John Anfinson. Other Bosse albums and ephemera have since emerged, and Anfinson is writing a history of the upper Mississippi, which will chronicle Bosse's known activities. It was Anfinson who first demonstrated precisely how Henry Bosse had used the photographs, actually tracing parts of them to refine his map of the river. He wrote, "Henry Bosse's photographs are more than art. They chronicle the first systematic effort to recast the upper Mississippi from a natural river into a modern commercial highway."

To fully appreciate Henry Bosse's genius, it is equally important to understand just how he participated in the expressive art world of his day. The consistency of *Views* more than suggests

The Seven-mile Beach in Sagami Province, from
Thirty-Six Views of Mt. Fuji, 1825–1832. Katsushika Hokusai
Woodblock print courtesy Rijksmuseum, Amsterdam

that he planned the impact of his photographic essay, as the Japanese artist Katsushika Hokusai had planned his *Thirty-six Views of Mount Fuji*. The artfulness of Bosse's images can be construed as an integral part of his intention. He set out to do more than map the Mississippi with a camera.

By the 1880s change was in the air. Three hundred years of industrial commerce had engendered staunch supporters and vocal critics. Adam Smith, Karl Marx, Henry David Thoreau, and Charles Darwin had each left their mark. Railroads were increasing the pace of daily life, as computers are today. At the time, photography appealed to English painters like Turner who were intrigued by its potential to render atmosphere and mood. Yet there remained the matter of color. Oil pigments in

easily portable lead tubes became available in the 1840s, just as clumsy photographic systems were emerging. This greatly facilitated plein air painting. Although slow and tedious, the lead tubes of oil had brilliant luminous colors, including the new, inexpensive ultramarine blues. For the French artists who were to lead the coming avant-garde, a core concept was emerging: to capture the fleeting impression that was held in the mind's eye, and to do so by rendering atmosphere and man's resonance with it. Vermeer had been on the track. Monet would come to call it "instantaneity." Conveying the power of a place and the moods of its people would prove, however, to demand more than Vermeer's enigmatic accuracy, more than Courbet's realism or Manet's painterly nuances. The interpreted color of dreams was required. Early on in the 1830s, with his *Thirty-six Views of Mount Fuji*, the innovative printmaker Hokusai realized the goal with Prussian blue on white.

Among schools of art, only Impressionism has enjoyed truly international appreciation. As a school of painting, it is a synthesis catalyzed by the appearance in Paris of certain Japanese woodblock prints. Creating wide appeal was undoubtedly the intention of Hokusai's Japanese publisher, although no one anticipated the eventual impact of *Views of Mount Fuji*. The newly developed Prussian blue ink, imported from Germany and very expensive in early nineteenth-century Japan, was employed to add cachet to Hokusai's seminal impressions of the lives and landscapes surrounding Fuji, a mountain sacred to the Japanese. The prints were an immediate success in Tokyo, sparking competitors like Hiroshige into action. Everywhere they were shown, they evoked appreciation. In a cycle of cultural exchange, Hokusai's *Views of Mount Fuji* found their way to Paris and Chicago as woodblock prints, and the innovative images became the talk of the day. The renowned Edmond de Goncourt of Paris discussed these prints in his journal. By the 1880s prominent banker Frederick Gookin was collecting Japanese prints in Chicago.

Facilitated by his style, Hokusai's message got through. The implication of his point of view — that human daily life naturally illuminates the land and the water — was not missed elsewhere. As his prints filtered into Paris in the 1840s and 1850s, others came to see at a glance that nature inhabited is a universal that is inherently spiritual. Through Hokusai's eye, man's resonance with nature reveals a world that is self illuminating and effervescent with feeling. Rendering this emotional reality, more than rendering realistically, is central to the establishment of an enduringly evocative impression. In Paris, Boudin and Monet caught on fast, and French plein air painting blossomed to heights rarely achieved in communication, the direct result of cross-cultural pollination. Nor was it long before the American James McNeill Whistler, then living in London, was painting the river Thames in moody blue monochromes. Whistler was said to be the first to paint the night, drawn to the blue mystery that veils the world from dusk to dawn as depicted in the color prints of Japanese masters.

Then as now, the entrenched artists resisted change, while younger artists embraced the new with enthusiasm. Evocative art was flowing into Europe and America, much of it with alien symbolism. Vivid woodblock prints, textiles, ceramics, things made for the common man, were appearing which had been made with far more thought and finish than the function demanded.

The 1880s found Oscar Wilde lecturing Americans on art for art's sake in New York, Detroit, Chicago, Minneapolis, Saint Paul, Rock Island, Dubuque, Saint Louis. Awakening each morning with a vow to be as perfect as his little, blue, Japanese vase, Wilde spent a year advocating the need for art in every life. Years later, in a conversation with Charles Freer, Whistler would come to impugn Wilde's originality, declaring that he, Whistler, had been aware of the significance of Japanese prints and had been incorporating their ideas in his own work since 1864.

When it was decided that the Army Corps would contribute to the United States Government Pavilion at the Columbian Exposition, Henry Bosse saw an opportunity to make the statement of a lifetime about the Mississippi River that he had come to love. Captain William Marshall of the Corps proposed a display for the exposition that was to be entirely photographic. Eventually, some models were included, but photographs would form the mainstay. Competition to be included was keen, and individual officers financed the photography of their own Army Corps programs.

These big fairs were pivotal cultural exchanges in the nineteenth century. Everyone wanted to be included. In America, as Chicago prepared for the upcoming 1893 Columbian Centennial, artistic excitement focused on the Japanese plan to build a replica of Byōdō-In Temple in Jackson Park. Japanese print collecting clubs formed. Elsewhere, the role that photography was to play at the exposition was being hotly debated. As the event drew near, even the young Alfred Stieglitz became embroiled in the dialogue. Eventually, his Photo-Secessionist movement would come to exist in direct reaction to his exclusion from the 1893 Columbian Exposition. In 1903, the year Bosse died, Stieglitz would be touting fine art photography in *Camera Notes* and curating exhibitions. Stieglitz and his pictorialists were once again left out of the 1904 Louisiana Purchase Centennial Exposition, in Saint Louis, where Henry Bosse's models and maps were displayed.

I like to ponder how Stieglitz might have reacted had he leafed through Bosse's album of cyanotypes. They certainly would have left an indelible impression: so real and definite, yet so expressive. Bosse demonstrated that the artistic photographer need not emulate the impressionistic painter's brush strokes; rather he must use the continuous tones of photography to achieve an equally enduring impression. Only a forward-looking perspective was required, one rooted in reality and centered on humanity as a force of nature. Nothing picturesque or symbolic is required, simply the moment of exposure compellingly rendered. Idea photography was emerging, and slowly, Stieglitz was getting the picture. The fuzzy focus of his Pictorialist movement would lose out to expressive photographs made by perceptive artists who were not trying to be European painters.

Because of the competition to be included in the Columbian Exposition, it seems likely that Henry Bosse produced these albums on his own. Cost was not the only concern; ambition would seem to have come into play. Henry Bosse wanted to exhibit more than an image or a glass plate, he wanted 169 images shown as a sequence. This many sheets of photographic paper tipped into a bound album would have been too thick and unwieldy, as the thirty-five-pound Bosse album in Rock Island demonstrates! The tough, thin paper used for cyanotypes suited his needs, as did the cyan blue itself. Once printed, the albums seem to have been Bosse's to allocate, hence the path leading to its discovery amid Alexander Mackenzie's personal papers. Other Bosse albums have found their way into the Woodward archive at the Mississippi River Museum in Dubuque, Iowa, and the Mayowood Library in Rochester, Minnesota.

To reflect on water and light, Henry Bosse used blue and white... and time. He labored a decade to create his enduring *Views on the Mississippi River*. With it, he left a lasting impression of the American experience, a map of his own Mississippi and a prophecy of the river to come. His vision ebbs and flows with the river. He navigates downstream, mapping what was to be gained and what would be lost, as engineers sought to control the water with wing dams of sticks and mud. Bosse meticulously records the shapes and surfaces, evoking a postmodern sense of transience as the pristine beauty of the land is engaged by intriguing webs of steel. His Mississippi blue images flow with the will of the water, ultimately acknowledging the environment itself as the source of the American dream.

Views on the MISSISSIPPI RIVER

between MINNEAPOLIS, Minn and ST. LOUIS, Mo.

under the direction of MAJOR A. MACKENZIE, Corps of Engineers U.S.A.

by H. Bosse, Draughtsman

1883-1891

From negatives taken and printed

From bluffs at Fountain City looking south

1.

Below the Falls of St. Anthony, Minneapolis, Minn.
1885.

6

From S. approach of Franklin Ave. Bridge, Minneapolis, Minn. looking up stream.
L. W. Jan. 1890.

14.

St. Paul, Minn
1885.

16.

River at St. Paul, Minn (from Daytons Bluff)
L.W. 1890.

Rocks and Dams below Frenchman's Bar
L.W. 1889.

34

From bluffs at Merrimac, Minn looking down stream.
1885.

37.

From head of Robinson's Rocks looking up stream
1891

41a.

Pine Bend
1885.

50 a.

Wingdams below Ninninger, Minn.
1891.

38

Diamond Bluff, Wis.
1889.

Mouth of Chippewa River.
1889.

From bluffs at Read's Landing, Minn. looking down stream
1885.

Wabasha, Minn
1889.

Channel behind Island 34 closed by Miss. Logging Co.
1889.

50

82

From bluffs at Fountain City, Wis. looking up stream.
1885.

Wingdams below Winona, Minn.
1889.

From bluffs at Trempealeau, Wis. looking down stream.
1885.

Queen's Bluff.
1885.

Bar in Front of La Crosse, Wis.
1891.

Mouth of Wisconsin River.
1885.

Crab Island Chain.
Rock Island Rapids 1891.

Front St. Davenport, Ia during High water 1888.

Front St.—Davenport, Ia. during High water 1888.

Second Avenue - Rock Island, Ill during high water.
1888.

Iowa State Penitentiary - Fort Madison, Ia.
1891.

Fort Madison, Ia.
1885.

137ᵈ

Riverfront – Fort Madison, Ia. 1885.

159 a

Head of Niota chute with closing dam.
1885

Causeway at Niota, Ill.
1885

Entrance to Guard Lock, – D. M. Rapids Canal

I. W. 1889

Outer faces of Dry Dock gates.
D. M. Rapids Canal 1894.

Middle Lock and Dry Dock.

D. M. Rapids Canal. 1884.

Lower Lock.
D. M. Rapids Canal.
1891.

156

Louisiana, Mo.
1885.

Raftboat "David Bronson."
1885.

171.

Raftboat in construction (Kahlke Bros. Boatyard, Rock Island, Ill.)
1891.

Boatyard of Kahlke Bros. Rock Island, Ill.
1891.

U. S. Dredge "Phoenix."
1885.

Cutting Brush & making Fascines.
1891.

Construction of Rock & Brush Dam.
L. W. 1891.

181.

Marshall Ave. Bridge, Minneapolis & St. Paul.
1889.

C. M. & St. P. R. R. Bridge at Hastings, Minn.
1885.

186.

C. B. & N. R. R. Bridge across mouth of St. Croix River.
1891.

192.

Old Ponton Bridge at N. McGregor, Ia.
1885.

193 a.

Old Ponton Bridge at Prairie du chien, Wis.
1885.

Wagon Bridge at Fulton, Ill.
1889.

Draw Span of C. & N. W. R. R. Bridge at Clinton, Ia.
1885.

201

U. S. Government Bridge at Rock Island, Ill.

High water 1888.

204.

Iowa Central R'y Bridge at Keithsburg, Ill.
1889.

205.

C. B. & Q. R. R. Bridge at Burlington, Ia.
1885

207.

Wabash R. R. Bridge at Keokuk, Ia.
1885.

C. B. & Q. Ry. Bridge at Quincy, Ill.
1885

Wagon Bridge at Winona, Minn.
1892.

N

List of Plates

THE CYANOTYPE PROCESS

from *Looking at Photographs: A Guide to Technical Terms* by Gordon Baldwin

THE CYANOTYPE PROCESS for making prints was invented by Sir John Herschel in 1842 and derived from his recognition of the light sensitivity of iron salts. A sheet of paper is brushed with solutions of ferric ammonium citrate and potassium ferricyanide and dried in the dark. The object to be reproduced, be it a drawing, negative, or plant specimen, is then placed upon the sensitized sheet in direct sunlight. After about a fifteen minute exposure, an impression has been formed, white where the light has not penetrated, on a blue ground. The paper is then washed in water, where oxidation produces the brilliant blue (cyan) that gives the process its name.

138

Bosse's World

The following articles project Henry Bosse's world, namely, the Midwest of the 1860s–90s. *Harper's Magazine* and the *Atlantic Monthly* were very influential then. In his 1875 *Atlantic Monthly* series, Mark Twain reveals the power of Old Man River to define every life along its banks. These articles by Twain preceded *Tom Sawyer* (1876), *Huckleberry Finn* (1885), and *Life on the Mississippi* (1833). The *Atlantic* articles were a smash hit. Twain had found his perfect protagonist, the river itself, forever mixing people and places, with its flow and chaos, and its terrifying muddy soul.

Then as now, news travelled fast, especially when propelled by gossip. Newspapers were more local, of course, yet in and around Chicago, the *Tribune* and the *Inter-Ocean* were widely read. As fate would have it, bare-knuckle champ John L. Sullivan and the utterly splendid Oscar Wilde converged on "Porkopolis" the same week in mid-February 1882, setting off a media riot about "The Two Esthetes!" Both articles are included to suggest the breadth of coverage that Wilde enjoyed nationally as he appeared in Chicago, Saint Louis, Rock Island, Dubuque, Minneapolis/ Saint Paul, New York, and Boston.

Also of interest are Henry Bosse's obituary and Corps of Engineers historian John O. Anfinson's overview of the upper Mississippi mapping project itself.

"The Body of the Nation"
[editorial, *Harper's Magazine*, February 1863]

But the basin of the Mississippi is the Body of the Nation. All the other parts are but members, important in themselves, yet more important in their relations to this. Exclusive of the Lake basin and of 300,000 square miles in Texas and New Mexico, which in many aspects form a part of it, this basin contains about 1,250,000 square miles. In extent it is the second great valley of the world, being exceeded only by that of the Amazon. The valley of the frozen Obi approaches it in extent; that of La Plata comes next in space, and probably in habitable capacity, having about eight-ninths of its area; then comes that of the Yenisei, with about seven-ninths; the Lena, Amoor, Hoang-ho, Yang-tse-kiang, and Nile, five-ninths; the Ganges, less than one-half; the Indus, less than one-third; the Euphrates, one-fifth; the Rhine, one-fifteenth.

It exceeds the extent of the whole of Europe, exclusive of Russia, Norway, and Sweden. It would contain Austria four times, Germany or Spain five times, France six times, the British Isles or Italy ten times. Conceptions formed from the river-basins of Western Europe are rudely shocked when we consider the extent of the valley of the Mississippi; nor are those formed from the sterile basins of the great rivers of Siberia, the lofty plateaus of Central Asia, or the mighty sweep of the swampy Amazon more adequate. Latitude, elevation, and rainfall all combine to render every part of the Mississippi Valley capable of supporting a dense population. As a dwelling-place for civilized man it is by far the first upon our globe. — EDITOR'S TABLE

Hannibal, Missouri. Henry Bosse
Photograph courtesy U.S. Army Corps of Engineers

Mark Twain
"Old Times on the Mississippi"
[*Atlantic Monthly*, January 1875]

WHEN I WAS a boy, there was but one permanent ambition among my comrades in our village [Hannibal, Missouri] on the west bank of the Mississippi River. That was, to be a steamboatman. We had transient ambitions of other sorts, but they were only transient. When a circus came and went, it left us all burning to become clowns; the first negro minstrel show that came to our section left us all suffering to try that kind of life; now and then we had a hope that, if we lived and were good, God would permit us to be pirates. These ambitions faded out, each in its turn; but the ambition to be a steamboatman always remained.

Once a day a cheap, gaudy packet [boat] arrived upward from St. Louis, and another downward from Keokuk. Before these events, the day was glorious with expectancy; after them, the day was a dead and empty thing. Not only the boys, but the whole village, felt this. After all these years I can picture that old time to myself now, just as it was then: the white town drowsing in the sunshine of a summer's morning; the streets empty, or pretty nearly so; one or two clerks sitting in front of the Water Street stores, with their splint-bottomed chairs tilted back against the wall, chins on breasts, hats slouched over their faces, asleep — with shingle-shavings enough around to show what broke them down: a sow and a litter of pigs loafing along the sidewalk, doing a good business in watermelon rinds and seeds; two or three lonely little freight piles scattered about the "levee"; a pile of "skids" on the slope of the stone-paved wharf, and the fragrant town drunkard asleep in the shadow of them; two or three wood flats at the head of the wharf, but nobody to listen to the peaceful lapping of the wavelets against them; the great Mississippi, the majestic, the magnificent Mississippi, rolling its mile-wide tide along, shining in the sun; the dense forest away on the other side; the "point" above the town; and the "point" below, bounding the river-glimpse and turning it into a sort of sea, and withal a very still and brilliant and lonely one. Presently a film of dark smoke appears above one of the remote "points"; instantly a negro drayman, famous for his quick eye and prodigious voice, lifts up the cry, "S-t-e-a-mboat a-comin'!" and the scene changes! The town drunkard stirs, the clerks wake up, a furious clatter of drays follows, every house and store pours out a human contribution, and all in a twinkling the dead town is alive and moving. Drays, carts, men, boys, all go hurrying from many quarters to a common center, the wharf. Assembled there, the people fasten their eyes upon the coming boat as upon a wonder they are seeing for the first time. And the boat is rather a handsome sight, too. She is long and sharp and trim and pretty; she has two tall, fancy-topped chimneys, with a gilded device of some kind swung between them; a fanciful pilot-house, all glass and "gingerbread," perched on top of the "Texas" deck behind them; the paddle-boxes are gorgeous with a picture or with gilded rays above the boat's name; the boiler-deck, the hurricane-deck, and the texas deck are fenced and ornamented with clean white railings; there is a flag gallantly flying from the jack-staff; the furnace doors are open and the fires glaring bravely; the upper decks are black with passengers; the captain stands by the big bell, calm, imposing, the envy of all; great volumes of the blackest smoke are rolling and tumbling out of the chimneys – a husbanded grandeur created with a bit of pitch-pine just before arriving at a town; the crew are grouped on the forecastle; the broad stage is run far out over the port bow, and an envied deck hand stands picturesquely on the end of it with a coil of rope in his hand; the pent steam is screaming through the gauge cocks; the captain lifts his hand, a bell rings, the wheels stop; then they turn back, churning the water to foam, and the steamer is at rest. Then such a scramble as there is to get aboard, and to get ashore, and to take in freight and to discharge freight, all at one and the same time; and such a yelling and cursing as the mates facilitate it all with! Ten minutes later the steamer is under way again, with no flag on the jack-staff and no black smoke issuing from the chimneys. After ten more minutes the town is dead again, and the town drunkard asleep by the skids once more.

My father was a justice of the peace, and I supposed he possessed the power of life and death over all men, and could hang anybody that offended him. This was distinction enough for me as a general thing; but the desire to be a steamboatman kept intruding, nevertheless. I first wanted to be a cabin-boy, so that I could come out with a white apron on and shake a table-cloth over the side, where all my old comrades could see me; later I thought I would rather be the deck-hand who stood at the end of the stage-plank with the coil of rope in his hand, because he was particularly conspicuous. But these were only day-dreams – they were too heavenly to be contemplated as real possibilities. By and by one of our boys went away. He was not heard of for a long time. At last he turned up as apprentice engineer or "striker" on a steamboat. This thing shook the bottom out of all my Sunday school teachings. That boy had been notoriously worldly, and I just the reverse; yet he was exalted to this eminence, and I left in obscurity and misery. There was nothing generous about this fellow in his greatness. He would always have a rusty bolt to scrub while his boat tarried at our town, and he would sit on the inside guard to scrub it, where we could all see him and envy him and loathe him. And whenever his boat was laid up he would come home and swell around the town in his blackest and greasiest clothes, so that nobody could help remembering that he was a steamboatman; and he used all sorts of steamboat technicalities in his talk, as if he were so used to them that he forgot common people could not understand them. He would speak of the "labboard" side of a horse in an easy, natural way that would make one wish he was dead. And he was always talking about "St. Looy" like an old citizen; he would refer casually to occasions when he was "coming down Fourth Street," or when he was "passing by the Planter's House," or when there was a fire and he took a turn on the brakes of "the old Big Missouri"; and then he would go on and lie about how many towns the size of ours were burned down there that day. Two or three of the boys had long been persons of consideration among us because they had been to St. Louis once and had a vague general knowledge of its wonders, but the day of their glory was over now. They lapsed into humble silence, and learned to disappear when the ruthless "cub-engineer" approached. This fellow had money, too, and hair-oil. Also an ignorant silver watch and a showy brass watch-chain. He wore a leather belt and used no suspenders. If ever a youth was cordially admired and hated by his comrades, this one was. No girl could withstand his charms. He "cut-out" every boy in the village. When his boat blew up at last, it diffused a tranquil contentment among us such as we had not known for months. But when he came home the next week, alive, renowned, and appeared in church all battered up and bandaged, a shining hero, stared at and wondered over by everybody, it seemed to us

that the partiality of Providence for an undeserving reptile had reached a point where it was open to criticism.

This creature's career could produce but one result, and it speedily followed. Boy after boy managed to get on the river. The minister's son became an engineer. The doctor's and the post-master's sons became "mud clerks"; the wholesale liquor dealer's son became a barkeeper on a boat; four sons of the chief merchant, and two sons of the county judge, became pilots. Pilot was the grandest position of all. The pilot, even in those days of trivial wages, had a princely salary – from a hundred and fifty to two hundred and fifty dollars a month, and no board to pay. Two months of his wages would pay a preacher's salary for a year. Now some of us were left disconsolate. We could not get on the river – at least our parents would not let us.

So, by and by, I ran away. I said I would never come home again till I was a pilot and could come in glory. But somehow I could not manage it, I went meekly aboard a few of the boats that lay packed together like sardines at the long St. Louis wharf, and humbly inquired for the pilots, but only got a cold shoulder and short words from mates and clerks. I had to make the best of this sort of treatment for the time being, but I had comforting day-dreams of a future when I should be a great and honored pilot, with plenty of money, and could kill some of these mates and clerks and pay for them.

"Oscar Wilde"
[*Chicago Inter-Ocean*, February 14, 1882]

MR. OSCAR WILDE made his aesthetic bow last evening to an audience that filled Central Music Hall in every seat. The obeisance was courteously preceded, accompanied, and briefly followed by applause, and then inattentive to the quickly commenced overture of a color artistically dull, all minds were bent upon the personel [sic] of the apostle of art. He was a pleasing, living water-color in two prevailing lines, black and white, with a crowning cloud – to follow the figure – of sunset glow in the shape of the much-described old-gold locks depending to the shoulders. The glazed shoes – to begin at the base – were not small – why should they have been when supporting that six-foot pedestal? – but the narrow length was richly accented by silk bows. Then came, in corresponding black, the silken hose, and above this the knee-ties of silk, again of ethiopic tint, and then the modest beginnings of black broadcloth, which made up the rest of an ordinary full-dress suit, barring a white vest. Of jewels, besides those unctuous ones of speech that fell from the sensuously full lips, a diamond cluster glowed on the expanse of shirt front, and a double fob of the latest order displayed stones of interblending hues, contrasted aesthetically on the ebony background. His collar was turn-down, and a beautifully opulent tie of white samite made a soft resting place for the abundant chin. The oval face in its golden setting of clinging hair was embodied mildness, benevolence, and ever and anon smiles. The auburn waviness, most marked at the forehead, imparted a suggestion of the effeminate, but the full and sonorous, if softly modulated, voice and the strong chin counteracted the impression.

HE HANDLED HIMSELF

with acknowledged perfection of self-possession, one arm now bent with hand at side, and the other resting with easy negligence on the stand or holding a roll of copy. The gently bended knee, now of this leg and then of that, secured good approxi-

mations to the beauty line in the silk-encased extremities. Evidently, the impression on the audience – whether by the mechanical or oratorical presentation of his subject, the "English Renaissance" – was quite pleasing from the start. As the local "points" were scored, the applause increased, and it was apparent long before the close that a recall to the stage would be the young and gifted, if somewhat too utterly utter, aesthetic's reward.

"In every great nation,"

SAID MR. WILDE IN BEGINNING,

"there is a certain amount of artistic power produced every year. You may use it or you may squander it, you may strew it on the sand of the desert or build for yourselves beautiful cities with it, but, believe me, you can never use it for any other purpose; and in the lecture which I have the honor to deliver before you to-night I wish to tell you of what we in England are doing now, searching in every city for those men and women who have power of design, knowledge and love of noble color and of imagination, and the schools of art that we have given them, and the work that we have done already, and the work that we propose to do. For this is the practical aim of our aesthetic movement, to produce among people that artistic temperament without which there is no creation of art. There is no understanding of art, there is not even an understanding of life, because such as your life is, so will your art be. If your life is noble and beautiful, noble and beautiful will your art be; but if a nation loves what is slanderous or foolish, their art will be an art all grotesque entirely, slander sneering at you from every gateway, malice mocking you from every arch.

"Great eras in the history of the arts" Mr. Wilde proceeded presently, are eras not of increased feeling, not of increased enthusiasm for art at all; they are eras for new technical improvement

143

primarily. They must begin with the workman, and with him alone. And so in our artistic movement in England we have been reacting against the empty, conventional workmanship of bad execution, and are producing poetry and painting; and, above all and more than this it is

THE FIRST MOVEMENT

which has brought the English craftsman and the artist together. Remember that if you separate one from the other, you do wrong to both; you isolate the artist from technical perfection, and you rob your hand-craftsman of all noble imagination, and of all spiritual motive. And so the greatest schools of art that the world has known – the school of sculpture at Athens, and the school of painting at Venice – found their source in a long succession of simple, earnest, and noble hand-craftsmen. It was the Greek father that taught the sculptor and the designer: it was the Italian painter on chests and furniture and household goods that taught the painters of Venice that noble and gorgeous color which is the secret of that great school.

"Perhaps you will tell me," said Mr. Wilde, in further development of the subject, "that you don't think much of the decorative arts, but that you are all devoted to the fine arts. Let me assure you that all the arts are fine arts, and that all the arts are decorative arts, too. The finest thing that Italian painting could do was to decorate the ceiling of the Pope's Chapel at Rome and the wall of a house at Venice; for Michael Angelo wrought the one and Tintoret the other. The little landscape that you hang over your mantel to-day or between your windows to-morrow is a far less glorious piece of work than those wide expanses of forest and field with which Bevocco has made beautiful the wondrous arcades of Pisa, and

that you use for a weight and keep in a little velvet case is a far less noble beast than that wild boar of Florence that foams out a fountain from beneath his tusks for the joy of the citizens."

"What did the Gothic artist of the thirteenth century think of the hand-craftsman? He found the best motives for his art always ready for him and always beautiful, in the daily work of the artificers he saw about him, as in those lovely windows in the Cathedral of Chartres. Real manufacturers those workers, with their hands and their heads, too, and very unlike many of our modern shopmen, who know very little about the things they sell one, except that they are charging us double its full value and thinking us a fool to buy it. You must seek out your workman, and you must give him, as far as possible, that right surroundings for a dyer. For the virtue of a workman is not his industry but his power to design. Design is no product of idle fancy: it is the result of accumulated habit and of delightful observation. All the teaching in the world will do no good in art unless you surround your workman with happy influences and with delightful things. It is impossible for him to have noble and beautiful color in his work unless he sees the lovely colors of nature displayed about him; impossible for him to have beautiful incidents and action in the design unless he sees in the world about him beautiful action and incident also."

A word painting, laid on in gorgeous colors, followed of the charms of Italian scenery, those factors of Italian artists, and the aesthete proceeded to point the moral thus, "So, we wish a school of design where the workman, as he walks the street, can see noble color and beautiful incident without the

DEPRESSING MONOTONOUS APPEARANCE

of too many modern cities. I have not seen an American city with any due attention to rock and river and mountain. Without a beautiful natural life, all the arts must die. I do not wish you to build a new Pisa, to bring back again the life and decoration of the thirteenth century; it is not merely impossible, it would be wrong. The circumstances with which you surround your workman must be those of the modern American life, because the designs that you have to ask from that workman are designs to make modern American life beautiful. The art that we must have is an art based on all the inventions of modern civilization to suit the requirements of nineteenth century life. Do you think for instance that I or those with me object to machinery? I tell you that we reverence it, reverence it when it does its proper work, when it relieves men from labor that is ignoble and labor that is shameful, but not when it seeks to do that which is only valuable when done by the living hand and noble imagination of some man or woman. Let us not mistake a means of civilization for the end of civilization. Some engines, a telegraph, and the like, are wonderful and noble, but their wonder and their nobility depends entirely on the value which we make of them. It is no doubt a great advantage to be able to talk to a man at the antipodes through a telephone [laughter at the odd pronunciation of the word, the first vowel being given the long sound as in teal duck], but it depends entirely on what the two men have to say to one another. If one of them

MERELY SHRIEKS ALONG

into the tube, and the other whispers folly into the wire I don't think that any of us are a bit the better for it. [Applause, during which Mr. Wilde takes artistically a sip of water.] A train that whirls the ordinary Englishman through Italy at a rate of forty miles an hour, and finally brings him home without any memory of that beautiful country except that he got a bad dinner at Verona or was cheated by courier at Rome – I don't think that this does much good to civilization or the man himself, but that swift legion of fiery-footed engines that bore to the ruins of your burning city the love, health and generous treasures of the world – that was as noble and as beautiful as any golden troop of angels that ever fed the hungry or clothed the naked in the antique time. [Loud applause.] As beautiful; all machinery may be beautiful. I cannot but think myself that all good machinery must be graceful, because the line of strength and the line of grace will grow together; and here in Chicago I have seen very little that is more beautiful than the machinery at your water works here. The rhythmic rise and fall of those long rods of polished steel, the stately orbit of that circling and giant wheel, were simply grand, but when I came out and saw your water tower,

THAT CASTELLATED MONSTOSITY

[great laughter, the aesthete sharing in it], that perforated pepper-pox stuck all over it [laughter], I felt amazed and grieved that you should so misuse gothic art, and that when you built a water tower you should try to make it as unlike a water tower as possible, to make it look like a mediaeval fortress. [Applause.] Give then, as I said, to your American workmen the opportunity of noble surroundings that you can yourselves create for them. Stately and simple architecture for your cities, bright and simple dress for your men and women – these are the conditions of artistic life, for the artist is concerned primarily not with any theory about life, but with visible life itself, a life that he sees and hears, that comes daily upon the eye and ear with all its joy and all its loveliness.

"But it is not enough to have a school of design in every large city; let it be a stately and a noble building; fill it with the best examples of the best decorative art in the world. Don't put your designer in a barren whitewashed room, as I have seen them in American schools of art, and tell him to design in

THAT JOYFUL ATMOSPHERE

[laughter], but give him the noblest possible surroundings, because you mean him to do the noblest possible work. He must always have about him specimens of the best decorative art of the world, so that you may be able to produce among your work-men a permanent standard of taste – a knowledge and appreci-ation of what is beautiful, something about which you can say to him, "Greek or Italians, English, Japanese wrought this so many years ago, but it is eternally young because it is eternally beautiful. Work in this sprit, and you will be right. Don't copy it, but work with the same love, with the same reverence, and with the same freedom and imagination." You must teach him color and design; you must show him how all beautiful colors are graduated colors, colors that always seem as if they were going to pass into the realm of another color, color without tone being merely like music without harmony – discord, and nothing else. Show your workman the quality of any beautiful work in nature, like the rose or any beautiful work in art, like an Eastern carpet and how its value depends entirely on the exquisite gradations of its color, one tone answering another like the chords in a beautiful symphony of music. Show him how the true designer does not draw out the design and color it afterward, but the designer must design in color,

GRADUATE IN COLOR,

and think in color. Show him how the best, most gorgeous stained glass in Europe, the glass of the thirteenth century – little we have left of it – and the most gorgeous Eastern tapestries, how it is the tone colors and the white glass, these two things that lend to each of them their own gorgeousness, the primary color being set in the white glass and worked into the tone colors, and so being like precious jewels set in dusky gold. And then, as regards design, show him how the designer must take a limited space and yet be effective widely. The Japanese artist thus shows the essence of good design with his little sprig or bird, making you think he is covering the whole of a fan or screen with beau-tiful designs merely because he knows the right place to put his supplementary touches.

"Especially enforce that good design depends on the texture of the material used, and the use you are going to put it to. In a certain American city – I haven't the courage to tell you the name – a beautiful young lady I saw painting away at a romantic moon-lit landscape on a large round dish, and another young and fair one covering dinner-plates with a wonderfully imaginative series of sunsets. [Laughter.] Let young ladies paint sunsets if they like, and moonlight if they dare, but don't let them

DO IT ON DINNER-PLATES.

[Great laughter.] Let them take canvas and paper for such work, not clay and china. Such heavenly scenes, let us not sup off them, neither send them down to the kitchen to be scrubbed and washed by the handmaid. [Applause.] The school of design would teach pupils all these things. We talked of Italian schools of painting, but they existed only in separate cities, and all different and all beautiful. No matter what New York and Philadelphia were trying to make in the art line, let Chicago carry out an independent course, because here are the primary conditions for a great artistic movement. For the noblest art one requires clear, healthy atmosphere, not murky, like the air of our English cities. One requires breath and strong physique. Idle and melancholy people never do anything in art. And lastly, you require individualism, the real essence of art, and a quality always most found in republics. Athens, Venice, Florence — there were no kings there; so their art was noble, natural, and sincere. A king's policy, as under Louis XIV, perpetrated the grotesque pile of the Tuileries. Every man is poor who cannot create. [Applause.] All around you here in this country and city, lie these conditions of success. For instance, in sculpture, what nobler models than where every man wears a frock coat, a tile hat, and an umbrella? [Laughter.] Let a searcher for models for his child's work go to the docks of any great city and see the toil, for I have never watched a man do anything useful, whether specially picturesque or not, who has not been at some moment of his work a graceful man. [Applause.] It is only the loafer and the idler who is as stupid and uninteresting to the artist as he is to himself. [Applause.] Or let him go to the university here and

SEE THE ATHLETIC SPORTS.

If in the simplest actions, as a woman draws up water from a well, an artist cannot find the noblest motive, he will never find it at all. The Greek carved gods and goddesses because he loved them, and the Goth loved governments and kings because they believed in them. Well, you don't care much for Greek gods and goddesses, and you are perfectly right, and I don't think you care much for kings either, and you are perfectly right, too. [Applause.] What you do love here are your own men and women, your own flowers and fields, your own hills and moun-

tains, and these are what your own art should represent for you. Don't imitate other nations; copy nothing. But of your American turkey you can make as charming decorative a bird as the Japanese their gray silver-winged stork. Let the Greek draw his griffin and dragon, your own deer will be the best for you. [Applause.] Golden rod, and astor and roses and all the flowers – what a wealth before your brush! You have quarries of marble whiter than the marble of Pentelicus, more varied in color than Greece ever had; but don't build great white houses of them. If you build in marble you must either carve it with beautiful decorations like those of the castles on the Loire, or you must fill it with beautiful sculpture, as did the Greek, or vary it

WITH COLORED MARBLES

as they did for all the palaces in Venice. Otherwise you had better build in simple red brick like your Puritan fathers, a style with no pretense, and really with some beauty.

All modern jewelry is commonplace. Gold is ready, in mountain hollow, for great improvements here. Gold is not only for wealth, but for the artificers skill. When such a one is found, encourage him, patronize him; tell him what you like best and let him materialize it – bird or animal, hound in the chase, the eagle in his flight, flower, the image of your friend you love; tell him to carve that for you; watch him as he beats out the gold into those beautiful little thin plates, delicate like the opening of the yellow rose itself, or draw it out into those lone wires that look like tangled sunbeams. [Applause.] Watch that workman, help him, cherish him, and you will have such lovely work from his hand as will be a delight to all of you. [Applause.]

"This is the spirit of our artistic movement, and this is the spirit in which we would wish to see you work. [Sensation]. Make the subject of your art all that is noble in men and women, the stately in your lakes and mountains, the beautiful in your flowers and in your life. We want to see you possess nothing in your houses that has not been a joy to the man who made it and is not a

JOY TO THE PEOPLE

who use it. We want to see you create an art made by the hands of the people. Do you like this spirit?" asked Mr. Wilde, with some impulsiveness, "as you have heard it, or not? Do you think it simple and strong, noble in its aim, and beautiful in its result? I can but think some of you here to-night do. [Faint applause.] Folly and slander have their own way for a little time, but for a little time only. You now know what we mean in England. You will be able to estimate what is said about us, its value and its motive. Let me read you the literary production of one of your Chicago citizens, a most interesting piece of criticism. Every morning since my arrival in America, and Chicago especially I have set aside a pleasant half hour for the perusal of your news-papers [applause] and yesterday morning as I was enjoying with your Chicago papers that usual and delightful luxury, I came across an astonishing account of the artistic movement in Eng-land about which I have told you as simply as I could to-night.

Then Mr. Wilde read, with much laughter, the clever satire, and proceeded:

"Well [laughter], I don't wish to reproach that wicked and imaginative editor. [Laughter.] I don't wish to strike daggers into his conscience, because I know from experience that the conscience of an editor is merely decorative [shouts of merri-ment, Oscar enjoying it hugely]; but at least I would like to think that, when you read, as you will read, many such produc-tions from the same eloquent pen, you will

you to-night, what we have done and what we wish you to do, what help you might give us by doing it. But you are as little likely to judge of a movement which England is giving so much of its strength and youth and power, by such a fellow as that as you would judge of the strength and splendor of sun or sea by the gust that dances in the beam, or the bubble that breaks on the wave. But – [with something of high scorn] let us leave this bad editor, and come back again to what is beautiful [much laughter]; let us come back again to art.

Mr. Wilde then maintained that national hatreds and many other ills are always strongest where culture is lowest and the arts most depressed. The test of a great nation is the closeness with which it stands by its great poets. Beauty and grace in all things are to be desired by nation and individual.

Children are familiarized with beauty by decorative art, hence the great attention bestowed on it in England. An instinct of the beautiful is succeeded, finally, as Plato said, in the child's mind by a rational choice of it. Industrious we must be, but industry without art is barbarism. By the drawer of water let an artistic water-pitcher stand. Decoration is the workman's expression of the joy he has in his work. William Morris tried to make each of his workmen an artist, i.e., a man. Keats reverenced only the Eternal Being, the memory of great men, and the principle of beauty. [Applause].

Then followed a sketch of how the speaker personally became interested in the movement, this branch including a really beau-tiful eulogy of old Oxford, where the new departure originated. Ruskin was represented as its god-father. Under his encourage-ment, young men, Wilde included, began laboring for the practically beautiful, and to this end even dug all winter in the adjacent swamps to throw up a bridge.

"Our enemies came and mocked us," said Oscar, "but we didn't mind it very much then, and don't mind it at all now." [Laughter and applause.]

Now, I don't want you to go to swamp-bridging, for I see before you more beautiful, for you, more natural decorations. There is no one of you here to-night who could not in a single month become master of some single decorative art that would be a joy to yourself and all your friends. There is nothing in life that the touch of art cannot ennoble. Commerce is not opposed to art. Genoa was built by its traders, Florence by its bankers, and Venice, loveliest of them all, by its noble and honest merchants; let America, with England, embrace the precedents. Then every leaf in your Titan forests shall yield to artistic permanence the beauty of its form and design, and no charming configuration of wild rose or briar, but will live forever in graven doorway or gateway of marble.

"Oscar Wilde"
[*Chicago Tribune*, February 14, 1882]

Oscar Wilde was announced to lecture last evening at Central Hall, and the great esthete had obtained so much free advertising hitherto that he was greeted with a crowded house. The lecture was announced for 8 o'clock, but long before that hour the impatient auditors began to crowd in, and the consequence was that early in the evening the lobby was crowded with anxious ticket-holders and buyers. It was not long before the significant legend of "standing-room only" was prominently posted, and yet the crowd kept thronging in. They were mainly nice people, too, although the audience viewed as a whole was not a dressy one. The crowd was so great that the lecturer was unavoidably obliged to postpone his appearance for some minutes to allow the bustle and confusion to subside. The great esthete was greeted with a magnificent audience of 2,000 people, who were orderly and appreciative. There was not the slightest suggestion of rowdyism or ridicule. Still there could be detected an evident feeling that the vast majority of Mr. Wilde's hearers came to see him, and not to hear him. The audience was passive, but respectful. It was even bored, at times, although the lecturer delivered the best and brightest address he has essayed in this country. It was easy to see that the best people in Chicago had gathered to see the "exponent of the best and highest art" without feeling the slightest real interest in what the speaker had to say. The audience was bright and appreciative, but they were cultured enough to know that the lecture would be a series of artistic platitudes without the slightest trace of artistic revolution. They found before the lecture was ended that the youthful speaker was imbued with the egotistical idea that the American public know nothing of art, as he pretended to teach them, and ended relating only axioms which have been the foundation of art for centuries. The lecture was partially new, or at least the old lecture was dressed up with certain allusions which possessed a local flavor, and evidently proceeded from a calculating business-manager. The effect on the audience can be summed up in the words of one who was heard to say: "I came to see Wilde, and I have seen him. I did not expect to learn anything and I did not." As luck would have it the reporter who interviewed Mr. Wilde also reported his lecture, and he learned that the esthete has a certain number of stock phrases always on his tongue's end, for much of the lecture was but a repetition of the interview which has already appeared in The Tribune.

on the stage entirely alone a few minutes after the appointed hour, waiting only until the great audience could secure seats. He was attired in a neat-fitting dress coat, low-cut white vest, showing the broad expanse of immaculate shirt front, with a broad white choker under a turn-down collar. He wore his conventional black trunks, tied at the knee with a small black bow, black silk stockings, showing a small and unshapely calf, with the usual low-cut pumps. His long hair was thrown back from his face, showing his ears more than ordinarily, and making him look less womanish than when he was seen in private. He stood well back from his reading-desk, displaying his form to advantage. His hands were gloved in white, the glove on the right hand having been drawn but half on. His attitude was easy, and the only act of nervousness was when he held his hands behind his back to take a pull at the half-drawn glove.

The lecturer began by saying that it was necessary above all to produce the artistic temperament, without which there could be no understanding of life itself. If life is noble and beautiful, art will be noble and beautiful. The great eras in the history of the arts are not eras of increased artistic feeling, but, primarily, of increased technical feeling – a feeling which must originate with the workman. It is above all the first movement which has brought the handicraftsman and the artist together. To separate them would rob the handicraftsman of all the best art he has ever known. It was the Italian painter who practiced his art

on old chests, and furniture, and house hold goods, who taught the Italian painter the glories which he subsequently developed. People may say that they do not like the decorative arts, but all arts are decorative arts. The Gothic artists of the thirteenth century, had the best motives for their art. All the teaching in the world would do no good unless the workman be surrounded with delightful things. It is impossible to have good workmanship unless the worker can see the beautiful things of Nature about him.

The scene which presented itself to the designer of the gothic school of Pisa, of Nino, of Pisaro, or any of his men, was elaborately described by the lecturer, who continued to contrast it with the sight which meets the eye of the modern designer. He went on to say that no machine-made ornaments should be tolerated. They were all bad, worthless, ugly. People should not mistake the means of civilization for the end. The steam-engine and the telephone depend entirely for their value on the use to which they are put. The speaker then went on to repeat his views almost word for word as printed in *The Tribune* interview, his peculiar pronunciation of the word telephone provoking prolonged laughter. He used the old simile of the Englishman whirled through Italy on a train running forty miles an hour and returning with only the memory of a bad dinner at Verona.

his local allusions. He said that at the time of the great fire the pouring out of the generous treasures of the world was as noble and beautiful as the works of any troop of angels who ever clothed the naked or fed the hungry in antique times. Here in Chicago the speaker had seen little that is more beautiful than the vast machinery of the Water-Works. In its vast beats right and left it was simple, grand, and natural. When he came out, however, he was shocked, for then he saw the water-tower, "a castellated monstrosity with pepper-boxes stuck all over it" [laughter], and felt amazed that any people could so abuse Gothic art and make the structure look not like a water-tower but like the tower of a medieval castle. The thing to be urged was bright and simple dress for the men and women, and stately and simple architecture for the cities, which is the foundation of art. The school of design in each city should be a building of stately and noble design. The best examples of decorative art should be before the designer that he may do the best work. He should have the examples of the best designers. They are eternal because externally beautiful. He should not copy them, but he should work with the same love, the same reverence, the same freedom of design which they abound in. Soft, shaded colors should be chosen, for color without tone is like music without harmony – a mere discord, and the dropping of a tint is like the loss of a measure, or a note even, in a grand symphony. Effect is the essence of good design. With a little spray of leaves and a little bird in flight the Japanese artist will make one think he has covered the whole surface of a plate, a fan, or a lacquered cabinet, simply because he knows exactly where to place each design. The speaker has seen in a school of design, in a city whose name he had not the courage to mention, a young lady painting an elaborate set of moonlight effects, and another of sunset work, on china. They might paint sunsets if they liked and moonlights if they dared, but let them not do it on dinner-plates. They had simply chosen the wrong material. A design which would be suitable for one material would not be suitable for another. The use to which an object is to be put should be a guide to the subject. Such subjects as these, if beautiful enough, should be handsomely framed and hung on walls. Soup should

not be eaten from them, nor should they be sent down to the kitchen twice a day to be scrubbed by a handmaid.

ALL GREAT ART IS COMPROMISED

in local schools and schools of particular cities. There never was an Italian school but schools of particular cities, and all the towns from Venice to Perugia had their peculiar school of art. The question is not what New York or Philadelphia is trying to do, but what will make a beautiful art for one beautiful city. The conditions of art are much more simple than people are prone to imagine. They consist chiefly in a clear, healthy atmosphere, a healthy, strong physique among men and women, and lastly, a sense of individualism about any man or woman. This the essence of art. It is the desire of man to express himself in the most beautiful manner possible. The grandest art of the world has always been the art of Republics. Too well is it known what kind of art the folly of Kings will impose on their people. Louis XIV, *le grand monarque*, gave to the world gaudy gilt furniture, writhing with the sense of its own ugliness, and not at all fit for use. The speaker did not want the rich to possess more beautiful things than the poor, but he did want the poor to possess them, and every man is poor who cannot create. All around lie these conditions. If an American were to ask the speaker for subjects, he would tell him to go first to the docks of any great city. He would tell him to go to the universities, to watch the young men starting for a foot-race, leaping from a boat, stopping to tie a shoe, or playing a game of ball. He should go to the meadow and watch the reaper with his sickle. If he cannot find subjects for his art in such things he never will find them at all. The audience did not care much for Greek gods and goddesses, and there they were right. They did not care much for Kings, either, and there they were right, too. What one has with him daily that should be, by the magic of the hand and the music of the lips, express gloriously to others. The American people

SHOULD NEVER IMITATE

unless they can make as good a design out of the American turkey as the Japanese out of his stork. The buffalo and the wild deer are the best for this country, for the people know them. To this country has been given natural marble more varied in color than any the Greeks ever had, but if a building is to be built it should be carved with beautiful designs, filled with sculptures or inlaid with beautiful colored marbles. Other wise, let people build with the red brick of the Puritan Fathers. The speaker knew of nothing more worthless in execution than modern jewelry. When a workman of artistic design could be found he should not be left in obscurity. He should be watched and cherished. This is the spirit of this new artistic movement.

The speaker then announced that he was in the habit of setting aside a pleasant half-hour for the perusal of the daily papers, a habit which had become a pleasant and delightful luxury in the morning. He then read an extract from an editorial in *The Tribune* comparing the schools of art represented by Wilde the esthete and Sullivan the pugilist with the comparison rather in favor of the latter. The extract was carefully selected from a long editorial, and went on to show that the art represented by Mr. Wilde consisted chiefly in substituting the ugly for the beautiful, ungainly pea-cocks and storks for birds, and filling houses with uncouth jugs, kettles, and monotonous fans, and plaques, clothing lean women in draperies without curves, and filling every garden with color-less conventionalities. The extract was applauded to the echo by the vast audience, while the comments were received with laughter.

The lecturer went on to say that he did not wish to reproach the wicked and imaginative editor, because he knew that the con-science of an editor is purely decorative. He would at least like to think that his audience would remember what he had told them of the spirit of his movement, and what help they might give to others. He would leave the bad editor and come back to the beautiful – come back to art.

The question was simply what art could do for the whole Nation. It was true that national hatred was always the strongest where culture was the lowest. There is no surer test of a nation than the discovery of how near it stands to its poets. The real influence of art consists in giving the mind the enthu-siasm to desire art in all things, for if it is not desired, it is not needed. The truths of art are not taught – they are revealed, and revealed only to natures which have made themselves receptive by the study and worship of all beautiful things. Art teaches us to bring up a child in the simple life of Plato's model city. Then when a child really grows up he learns that industry without art is barbarism. Even the pitcher which goes to the well should at least be pretty. No better definition of what is meant by the word "artist" could be given than the saying of Mr. Morris, "I have tried to make each of my workers an artist, and when I say an artist I mean a man." Keats said that he had no reverence for anything but the eternal being, the memory of great men, and the principle of beauty. That is the great under-lying principle of the English renaissance.

Mr. Wilde then told of the birth of his dream to create an artistic revolution in England. He was one day walking down High Street at Oxford with a noisy party of undergraduates on their way to cricket, tennis, and boating, when they met Mr.

Ruskin proceeding to his lecture. Some of them returned and listened to him while he told them how wrong it was that the brains and brawn of England should be wasted in athletic sports. With the party, then, he set to work on a mission of good, building a road through a swamp for the convenience of the neighboring villagers. None of the party faltered, and from this beginning their attention was turned to loftier aims, of which the speaker had become the exponent. He did not ask the young men and women of America to build roads through swamps, but he did wish to suggest that there was not one in the audience who could not in a month become master of some simple decoration.

In conclusion the speaker said that the commercial spirit was not opposed to art, for commercial men had built the most artistic cities of the world. The nation which absorbs the artistic spirit into its heart will create such treasures as have never been seen before. Above all there should be a sympathetic feeling for young artists, who can often be sustained and inspired by a word. The voices which have their dwelling in sea and mountain are not alone the chosen music of liberty, there being other messages which will teach the secret of all splendid imaginings, the secret of all true loveliness.

A SOCIETY EVENT

Mr. Wilde was entertained yesterday afternoon by Mr. and Mrs. Franklin MacVeagh at their residence, No. 1823 Michigan Avenue, in a very pleasant manner. At half-past 1 o'clock a lunch party was given in Mr. Wilde's honor, and there were present Mr. and Mrs. Whitehouse, Mr. and Mrs. Leslie Carter, the Misses Alice and Kittie Arnold, Miss Gardner, Miss Hoteling, Mr. Ord, Mr. Wilde, and Mr. and Mrs. MacVeagh.

After lunch, Mr. MacVeagh drew Mr. Wilde out, and he talked very pleasantly on the subjects of dress, dancing, etc. He said that artificial flowers should never be worn; all ladies might wear lilies, but only an Oriental beauty could wear the sunflower. One dress made by an artist, he said, was worth five dresses made by a dressmaker. In speaking of dancing he said he believed that the minuet would be revived. When he gave large balls in England they used to dance the minuet and other old dances in the costumes of the time, and in this connection he stated that appropriate costumes should always be worn. He was told the Americans thought they danced better than the English, and he acknowledged this to be a fact. In speaking of beautiful women he said he believed that Mme. Christine Nilsson and Mrs. Langtry were the most beautiful women in the world. His conversation was very pleasant and agreeable, and he said many sensible and witty things.

At 3 o'clock Mr. Wilde was tendered a reception, and a number of ladies and gentlemen were present during the afternoon. As the guests entered the parlors they were introduced to the great esthete, and he had a pleasant word and a smile for all. He wore an olive velvet coat, baggy grey breeches, a brick-red necktie, and a handkerchief of the same shade peeped out of the upper pocket of his coat. His long hair was matted and tangled, and detracted much from his general appearance, but this drawback was lost sight of when he smiled and talked. The ladies present displayed a number of esthetic toilets.

Mr. Wilde will be given a dinner this afternoon at the residence of Mrs. H. O. Stone, and will meet a few of her friends in the evening.

From *The Life of James McNeill Whistler*
E. Robins and J. Pennell
[Lippincott, 1911]

NOCTURNES. 1872–1878: Whistler was the first to paint the night. The blue mystery that veils the world from dusk to dawn is in the colour-prints of Hiroshige. But the wood-block cannot give the depth of darkness, the method makes a convention of colour. Hiroshige saw and felt the beauty and invented a scheme by which to suggest it on the block, but he could not render the night as Whistler rendered it on canvas.

Though colour prints suggested the Nocturnes, they were only the suggestion. Whistler never copied Japanese technique. But Japanese composition impressed him – the arrangement, the pattern, and at times the detail. The high or low horizon, the line of a bridge over a river, the spray of foliage in the foreground, the golden curve of a falling rocket, the placing of a figure on a shore, the signature in the oblong panel, show how much he learned. He abandoned the Japanese convention in a few years, but he never gave up, he developed rather, what he always spoke of as the Japanese method of drawing. He translated Japanese art – translate is the word – though he said that he "carried on the tradition." His idea was not to go to the Japanese as greater than himself, but to learn what he could from them and make another work of art.

"Poisoned at Meal"
[*Rock Island Daily Argus*, December 14, 1903]

Henry Bosse Made Critically Ill By Eating Canned Asparagus
AT HIS HOME YESTERDAY
Physicians Work Over Him Several Hours Before
Bringing Him Past Danger Point.

HENRY BOSSE, draughtsman at the United States river engineers office, was poisoned yesterday at his home on Seventh Avenue by canned asparagus, and for a time his life was despaired of.

Lunch was served at 1 o'clock and in part consisted of asparagus, of which Mr. Bosse is very fond and of which he partook freely.

Shortly after rising from the table he complained of feeling ill and went to his room to lie down.

PHYSICIANS CALLED IN

In a few minutes he was seized with terrible pains, when physicians were summoned and found Mr. Bosse in a critical state, and it was only after they had labored over him several hours that they pronounced him out of danger.

"Causes His Death"
[*Rock Island Daily Argus*, December 15, 1903]

Bowel Trouble Results Fatally to Henry Bosse Last Evening.
PASSES AWAY AT HOSPITAL
Where He Had Been Taken to be Operated on –
Funeral Thursday

HENRY BOSSE, poisoned by eating canned asparagus Sunday, and thought to have been out of danger yesterday afternoon, was seized with a relapse last evening and removed to St. Anthony's hospital where he expired at 7 o'clock in the evening just as the physicians had began to operate on him. While the poison produced a deathly sickness, a council of physicians late in the afternoon diagnosed the trouble as obstruction of the bowels due to intestinal misplacement, and determined that his only chance lay in a speedy surgical operation. But Mr. Bosse hardly survived the preparations.

Deceased was one of the cultured, well-known and highly regarded men of the city, having served for a quarter of a century as chief draughtsman in the office here of the government engineering department. He was born on his father's estate, Sonnendorf, in Prussian Saxony, November 13, 1844, where his earlier years were spent. Besides classical studies, he familiarized himself with engineering and art.

Mr. Bosse was the grandson of Count Neithardt von Gueisenau, the Prussian general of the Napoleonic wars, to whose strategy much of the credit is given by historians for the overthrow of the Corsican leader. Twenty-nine years ago Mr. Bosse came to the United States.

FIRST LOCATES IN CHICAGO

He first located in Chicago, remaining there four years, when he was appointed to the position in the river engineering department that he continued to occupy until his death. Mr. Bosse is survived by his widow (nee Miss Hulda Thiele, of Davenport), to whom he was married eight years ago.

The funeral services will be held at deceased's late home, 2912 Seventh avenue, at 2 o'clock Thursday afternoon. Interment will be in Oakdale cemetery, Davenport.

From *Henry Bosse's Views of the Upper Mississippi River*
John O. Anfinson
[U.S. Army Corps of Engineers, 1996]

HENRY BOSSE'S photographs are more than art. They chronicle the first systematic effort to recast the upper Mississippi from a natural river into a modern commercial highway....

Before the Corps could begin remaking the upper Mississippi River, it needed to understand the river better. So during the winter of 1877–78, Major Francis U. Farquhar, the Rock Island District commander, directed his engineers to synthesize all the earlier river maps into a general map of the upper Mississippi from St. Anthony Falls to Grafton. When completed, the new map included 26 sheets. Not satisfied with the map's detail and coverage, Farquhar asked the Chief of Engineers for $60,000 to resurvey the river, and on July 8, 1878, the chief approved.

To draw the new map, Major Farquhar needed a talented draftsman. Farquhar had been the St. Paul District Engineer from 1873 to 1878, and Bosse had worked for St. Paul in 1875 and maybe longer. Knowing Bosse's skills, Farquhar probably asked him to move to Rock Island.

Between 1878 and 1879, the Engineers conducted their survey. They sounded the river to find its deepest and most continuous channel. They calculated the drainage areas of its tributaries, figured its elevation at low and high water and its slope between towns. Finally, they completed a twenty-seven-page map of the upper river between St. Paul and Grafton illustrated by Bosse and his assistant, A. J. Stibolt. The government did not publish the map until 1887–1888. By participating in the survey and drawing the maps, Bosse must have become intimately familiar with the geometry of the river's landscape and all of its moods.

While Major Farquhar initiated the 4 ½-foot channel project, Alexander Mackenzie would become its principal architect. Arriving in June 1879 as a Captain, he remained in charge of the Rock Island office for sixteen years. Over these years, he formed a close friendship with Bosse. Mackenzie knew the river well before going to Rock Island. He had been born near the river at Potosi, Wisconsin, on May 25, 1844 (less than six months before Bosse,) and had attended grammar and high school in the river port of Dubuque, Iowa. In 1860 Mackenzie entered the United States Military Academy and graduated four years later at the top of his class.

To achieve the 4½-foot channel, the Corps would have to narrow and constrict the river. They did this by building wing dams and closing dams. Long, narrow piers of rock and brush, wing dams jutted into the river from the main shoreline or from the bank of an island. The Engineers placed the wing dams in a series along one or both sides of the channel to reduce its width at low water, which usually occurred in the late summer and fall. By narrowing the river, they increased its velocity (like the nozzle of a garden hose being tightened down,) enabling the river to cut through sand and debris in the main channel. Moving faster, the river carried more sediment, some of which settled out in the calmer waters behind or between the wing dams. Within a few years, the space between the dams filled with sand and plants. In this way, the Engineers constricted the river, gradually moving its banks inward. Through his photographs, Bosse detailed every phase of this process.

Wing dams depended upon the volume of water in the river. Without enough water, they could not scour the channel. Hundreds of islands divided the natural river, dispersing its waters into innumerable side channels and sloughs. By dividing the river, they reduced the flow available for the main channel and thereby its depth. To deliver more water to the main channel, the Engineers built closing dams. These dams ran from the shore to an island or from one island to another. While the river could flow over them when high, for the most of the year the dams directed water to the main channel.

As wing dams and closing dams increased the main channel's velocity and volume, they accelerated bank erosion. Wing dams, by forcing the river away from one shore and against the other, were especially responsible. To stop the erosion, the Corps armored hundreds of miles of shoreline with brush mats and stone.

Channel constriction did not eliminate the need for dredges and snagboats. When Captain Mackenzie took command of the Rock Island office in 1879, the snagboat *General Barnard* was the District's only major work boat for the upper Mississippi River. To vigorously pursue the channel constriction project, he began arguing for a government fleet. By 1882 Mackenzie had acquired four towboats, three steam-launches, fifty-five stone barges, and "the necessary complement of quarter-boats, pile-drivers, etcetera." In addition, he added the snagboat *J. G. Parke* and the dredge *Phoenix*. Bosse would draw some of the boat plans, and as Corps work boats became essential to the Engineers' river improvement strategy, he photographed much of the fleet.

Neither dredging nor channel constriction worked at the Des Moines and Rock Island Rapids. The Des Moines Rapids extended more than eleven miles upstream from Keokuk, Iowa, and the Rock Island Rapids, composed of seven chains of rock, stretched nearly 14 miles from Rock Island upstream to LeClaire, Iowa.

During low water both rapids became nearly impassable, forcing larger steamboats to transfer their goods and passengers to smaller boats.

As early as 1829, the government had considered improving these rapids for navigation. While the Corps evacuated some rock from the Rock Island Rapids between 1854 and 1856, it did not seriously attack this trouble spot until after the Civil War. The Engineers began removing rock again in the fall of 1867, and proceeded chain by chain until, in 1886, they had excavated most of the channel to a minimum width of 200 feet and a minimum depth of four feet. While this channel made the Rock Island Rapids more navigable, they were still treacherous.

Rather than assault the Des Moines rapids directly, the Engineers decided that it would be easier to build a canal paralleling the river. Begun on October 18, 1867, the project required ten years to complete. Opened in 1877, the canal served the upper Mississippi River traffic until the fifty-mile-long reservoir formed by Keokuk and Hamilton Water Power Company lock and dam, completed in 1913, flooded it. Bosse's photographs of the canal and locks demonstrate his ability to present complex engineering subjects gracefully.

His images of railroad and wagon bridges further reveal this talent. Major Mackenzie undoubtedly directed Bosse to photograph these bridges because their piers created a new peril for steamboats. Mackenzie regularly complained about the problem to his superiors. "I would repeat my urgent recommendation made in all previous reports," he wrote in his 1884 report to the Chief of Engineers, "that the Government shall take such action as will relieve the navigation interests of the great tax now imposed on them by the failure of bridge companies to properly facilitate navigation through their bridges." Mackenzie kept making this plea because steamboats driven by strong winds or caught in the tricky currents created by the piers kept running into the bridges. And the number of bridges was growing quickly.

The first two railroad lines had reached the upper river in 1854, and over the next four years seven more established rail heads on the river's east bank. The Civil War delayed railroad expansion, but between 1865 and 1869, three railroad lines crossed the Mississippi into Iowa. By 1880, thirteen railroad bridges spanned the upper river.

Railroads held many advantages over waterway transport. Railroads moved freight quicker, giving their users greater flexibility in responding to market changes. Rail lines were generally shorter and more direct, and they reached deep into areas that no river could serve. Trains ran when the river was high or low, and they ran when the cold of winter froze it for the most part, they ran throughout the year. Consequently, the river lost grain and passenger traffic to railroads even as the Corps improved the river.

By the 1890s, the timber rafting remained the only significant river traffic. So it was not surprising that Bosse photographed raftboats and lumber yards. Commercial lumbering began in western Wisconsin and Minnesota in the late 1830s and grew rapidly in the 1840s and 1850s. Vast forests of white pine stood in Wisconsin and Minnesota. By one estimate, one-sixth of the white pine west of the Appalachian Mountains stood in the Chippewa River valley alone. Stout but easily cut and milled, it became the primary building material for most Midwestern cities. And white pine had another unique quality, unlike maple, oak and other hardwoods, it floated.

Timber products dominated the upper river's commerce from the 1870s to the first decades of the twentieth century. They comprised the greatest quantity of merchandise shipped on the river, and they accounted for most of the total value of the goods that moved on it. More than passenger traffic or grain hauling, timber shipping would justify federal spending on river improvements. Bosse undoubtedly photographed the timber industry to show how important the river and the Corps' work still were to the Midwestern economy.

Bosse and Mark Twain present vivid images of the rafting industry, although from differing perspectives. Returning to the river in 1882 after a long absence, Twain compared life on the river to his experience some thirty years earlier. "Up in this region," he observed, "we met massed acres of lumber-rafts coming down – but not floating leisurely along in the old-fashioned way, manned with joyous and reckless crews of fiddling, song-singing, whiskey-drinking, breakdown-dancing rapscallions; no, the whole thing was shoved swiftly along by a powerful sternwheeler, modern fashion; and the small crews were quiet, orderly men, of a sedate business aspect, with not a suggestion of romance about them anywhere." Yet, Bosse's photographs of the raftboats are decidedly romantic.

Timber shipping on the upper Mississippi River fell with the white pine forests of western Wisconsin and northern Minnesota. By 1909, mills on the river generated only one-quarter of the lumber they had eight years earlier. Of more that one hundred raftboats plying the river in 1893, fifty remained in 1904, and only four in 1912. In 1915, the Ottumwa Belle guided the last lumber raft down the Mississippi from Hudson, Wisconsin, to Fort Madison, Iowa.

REFERENCES

John O. Anfinson, "Henry Bosse and the Mississippi's Passage into the Age of Industry," *History* (Ramsey County Historical Society), winter 1992–93, pp. 4–9.

John O. Anfinson, "Portraits of Old Man River," *Minnesota Volunteer*, November–December 1991, pp. 32–49.

Gordon Baldwin, *Looking at Photographs: A Guide to Technical Terms* (Los Angeles: J. Paul Getty Museum, 1991).

Julie K. Brown, *Contesting Images: Photography and the World's Columbian Exposition* (Tucson: University of Arizona Press, 1994).

Claude Debussy, *Prélude à l'après-midi d'un faune*, London Symphony Orchestra, conducted by André Previn (EMI Records, 1979).

Ron Deiss, *Views on the Mississippi: The Landscape Photography of Henry Peter Bosse* (Rock Island, Ill.: Army Corps of Engineers, 2001).

Matthi Forrer, *Hokusai* (New York: Rizzoli, 1988), pp. 264–67.

Thomas Lawton and Linda Merrill, *Freer: A Legacy of Art* (New York: Abrams, 1993), pp. 54, 64.

Lloyd Lewis and Henry J. Smith, *Oscar Wilde Discovers America* (New York: Harcourt Brace, 1936).

Mark Neuzil and Merry Foresta, *Views on the Mississippi: The Photographs of Henry Peter Bosse* (Minneapolis: University of Minnesota Press, 2001).

William C. Seitz, *Monet* (New York: Abrams, 1983), p. 12.

John Whitehead, *Mississippi Minnesota* (St. Paul: Twin Cities Public Television, Inc., 1992). Video production.

Gary Zabel, editor, *Art and Society: Lectures and Essays by William Morris* (Boston: George's Hill Publications, 1993).

The Bosse Albums

NEARLY 900 PHOTOGRAPHIC PRINTS by Henry Peter Bosse are included in the archives of the U.S. Army Corps of Engineers at Rock Island, Illinois and Saint Paul, Minnesota; in the Mayo Foundation Library in Rochester, Minnesota; with the Mississippi River Museum of Dubuque, Iowa; and in the Mackenzie album sold at Sotheby's. More than 345 separate negatives and several printing techniques are involved. Their nuances reveal the depth of Henry Bosse as an expressive artist exploring a new medium. While some prints are black and white, the vast majority are oval-masked cyanotypes bound into albums. Most are individually numbered and captioned with pen and ink by a hand presumed to be that of Henry Bosse himself. Occasionally, a number is extended with *a*, *b*, *c*, or *d*. A few prints are captioned without a number, while others have no writing on them at all. The Dubuque album, in two volumes, was recently numbered with a different system. No two albums are identical, nor does any one album contain all the images.

Based on Bosse's own "List of Views" from the Rock Island album, Bob Wiederaenders, archivist for the Dubuque Historical Society, is compilng an inventory of Bosse's *Views on the Upper Mississippi River* from the various albums, plus unbound prints discovered with them. This inventory is generally organized from north to south. Loose prints without numbers are also placed geographically. The dates of the negatives span 1883−1893.

COMPLETE LIST OF PLATES IN THE MACKENZIE ALBUM

VIEWS

1. Below the Falls of St. Anthony, Minneapolis, Minn. 1885

2. Old Steamboat Landing at Minneapolis, L.W. [low water] 1890

4. From bluffs opposite Riverside Park, Minneapolis Minn., looking
*   upstream, Jan. 1892*

6. From S. approach of Franklin Ave. Bridge, Minneapolis, Minn.
*   looking up stream, L.W. Jan.1890*

10. Fort Snelling. 1889

12. Soldier's Home and mouth of Minnehaha Creek. 1889

14. St. Paul, Minn. 1885

16. River at St. Paul, Minn. (from Dayton's Bluff) L.W. 1890

18. From foot of Dayton's Bluff, St. Paul looking down stream. 1885

21. Rocks and Dams below Frenchman's Bar, L.W. 1889

22. Wingdams at head of Pigs Eye Island. 1889

23b. *Pig's Eye Island. 1889*

24a. *Wingdams above S. St. Paul. 1890*

26. *From wagon road at S. St. Paul looking up stream. 1891*

27. *From wagon road at S. St. Paul looking down stream. 1891*

29. *Natural deposit & growth of willows above & below Dam 212. 1891*

31. *From Landing at Newport, Minn. looking up stream. 1889*

32. *From bluffs at Merrimac, Minn. looking up stream. 1889*

33. *From bluffs at Merrimac, Minn. looking up stream. L.W. 1891*

34. *From bluffs at Merrimac, Minn. looking down stream. 1885*

35. *From bluffs at Merrimac, Minn. looking down stream.* [1889]

36. *From bluffs at Merrimac, Minn. looking down stream. 1891*

37. *From head of Robinson's Rocks looking up stream. 1891*

38. *From middle of Robinson's Rocks looking up stream. 1885*

38a. *Wingdams opposite Robinson's Rocks. 1891*

39. *From foot of Robinson's Rocks looking up stream. 1891*

40b. *From foot of Robinson's Rocks looking up stream. 1891*

41a. *Pine Bend. 1885*

42. *Pine Bend. 1891*

45. *From bluffs at Pine Bend looking down stream. 1891*

45[a]. *From bluffs at Pine Bend looking down stream. 1891*

47. *From Quarry at foot of Boulanger Slough looking up stream. 1891*

48. *From Quarry at foot of Boulanger Slough looking down stream. 1891*

50a. *Wingdams below Ninninger, Minn. 1891*

51. *From bluffs at Franklin's Coulee looking down stream. 1891*

52a. *Wingdams in bend below Ninninger, Minn. 1885*

53. *Bar above Hastings. 1889*

55. *Bar and wingdams below Hasting, Minn. 1891*

57. *Mouth of St. Croix River.. 1885*

58. *Prescott, Wis. 1885*

59. *Diamond Bluff, Wis. 1889*

60. *Redwing, Minn. and Barn Bluff. 1891*

62. *Breakwater at Stockholm, Wis. 1889*

63. *Breakwater at Lake City, Minn. 1889*

64. *Mouth of Chippewa River. 1885*

65. *Mouth of Chippewa River. 1889*

67a. *From bluffs at Read's Landing, Minn. looking down stream. 1885*

67b. *From bluffs at Read's Landing, Minn. looking down stream. 1889*

68. *Read's Landing, Minn. 1889*

69. *Wabasha, Minn. 1889*

70a. *From foot of Dam 113 looking up stream, L.W. 1889*

70b. *From Tee-pe-o-ta Point looking up stream. 1889*

71. *Channel behind Island 34 closed by Miss. Logging Co. 1889*

72c. *From bluffs at Alma, looking up stream. 1891*

75b. *Alma, Wis. 1889*

76. *Foot of W. Newton Chute. 1889*

77. *Boom at Minneiska. 1889*

78. *Minneiska, Minn. 1889*

78a. *Minneiska, Minn. 1885*

79a. *Foot of I'd 50. 1889*

80. *Chimney Rock Bar. 1889*

81. *Richtman's Quarry at Fountain City, Wis. 1891*

82. *From bluffs at Fountain City, Wis. looking up stream. 1885*

82a. *From bluffs at Fountain City, Wis. looking down stream. 1885*

86. *From river at Fountain City, Wis. 1891*

88. *Wingdams below Winona, Minn. 1889*

90. *From bluffs at Trempealeau looking up stream. 1885*

91. *Trempealeau, Wis. 1885*

92. *From bluffs at Trempealeau, Wis. looking down stream. 1885*

93. *Queen's Bluff. 1885*

94. *Dakota, Minn. 1891*

162

Acknowledgments

I WANT TO THANK the following
individuals for their interest in Henry P. Bosse,
and especially for their critical comments on my introductory essay:
Sally Larsen, John Anfinson, Priscilla Farnham, Charles Stuckey, John Rohrbach,
Merry Foresta, Weston Naef, John Szarkowski, Maria Morris-Hambourg,
Beth Gates-Warren, Denise Bethel, James Enyeart, John Wood, Sarah Greenough,
Sandra Phillips, Joan Mirviss, Michael Malcolm, Peter Jones, Simon Lowinsky,
Steve and Betsy Lichtenberg, Dan and Mary Solomon, Charles Isaacs, Paul Sack,
David Mahoney, Bill Cole, Chris Cardozo, Gary Albright, Darren Quintenz,
the late Merrily Page, Tom Akawie, MaryAnne Kuzniar, Jeff Walba,
George Scrivani, Mike Conner, Ron Deiss, John Thompson,
Frank Piehl, Bob Wiederaenders, Mark Neuzil,
Raymond T. Tatum, Tom Weir, Jeff Rosenheim.